The Persistence of Memory

The Persistence of Memory

Poems by

Steven Deutsch

Cover design by Shay Culligan

ISBN: 978-1-952326-05-9

Kelsay Books
502 South 1040 East, A-119
American Fork, Utah, 84003

For my wife, Karen,
for her help and encouragement.

~

With thanks to my poetry group for friendship and advice,
Sarah Russell who helped organize
this collection, and Lisa McMonagle who helped with many
versions of these poems.

Acknowledgments

Algebra of Owls: Zippo

Better Than Starbucks: Comfort

Blue Nib: How We Fail

Borski Press: The Dying of the Light

Broadkill Review: Fumarole

Eclectica: As One, For Nothing at All, Lion's Breath, The Way We Are Now, Urban Redevelopment

Flashes of Brilliance: Estranged, Spendthrift

Ghost City Review: Leroy

Linden Avenue Literary Journal: DNA

Locust: Taxi

Loyalhanna Review: Your Birthday Would Be this Week

Misfit Magazine: I Remember November 1963, The Home Front—3/16/68

Mojave River Review: First Kiss

Muddy River Poetry Review: Stan

Nixes Mate Review: Breakdown

Panoply: Archangel

Pure Slush, Seven Deadly Sins (Envy): Sex Appeal

San Antonio Review: Reunion

Softblow: A Death in the Family, At the Bay

The Drabble: A Retirement, Monkey Bars, What I Had Forgotten

Street Light Press: Untethered

Third Wednesday: Pyre, Sam and Saul, Song

Word Fountain: At the Edge, The Year We All Got Cancer

Contents

And there it is,
something sweet
from who knows where—
an arrival as unsuspected
as finding,
upon your doorstep,
something old and dear
you never knew you'd lost.

I

Monkey Bars

The old playground.
was fenced off years ago.
The rusted frames
of sliding pond
and see-saw
stand silhouetted in the setting sun.
The swing set—seatless now—
where young mothers
took their toddlers
on weekday afternoons,
and where we,
barely teenage,
first made acquaintance with longing.

We fought on the monkey bars
for world domination,
screeched like chimpanzees
and beat each other silly.
We ranked each other out
in words we hardly understood
and screamed,
"I'll murder ya,"
"I'll break ya neck,"
at the top of our lungs
until one day we did.

Zippo

I was six when
the corner hardware store caught fire.
We were chased from our apartment
by smoke and heat
and the staccato pop of flammables bursting.

I remember the sudden burn
of winter and my mom's blue lips,
as my dad, muttering and cursing,
tried to coax
the old Packard Eight to life.

The world outside
was ice and ash.
Sirens bawled and
yellow-jacketed men
wielded axes like arms
and strained against hoses
struggling to break free.

Mom told me years later
that she had wrapped me in an old fur.
She said it was the coldest night
of the year, and only the heat
from the car kept us from frostbite.
Try as I might
I can't remember that.

I remember I shared the back seat
with my brother—
thirteen and the source of all knowledge—
and that he'd found a cigarette lighter that week
and showed me how to make a fire
of rags and paper,
and that his terrified face
flickered all night in the flamelight.

First Kiss

Back in the early '60s
you didn't need a crystal ball
to tell the neighborhood
was going to hell.
Even the children knew—
acquiring a wariness
like some sixth sense for city kids.

In the summer of '62,
I sat with her
for as long as the lengthened
evenings allowed,
on the stone steps
that served as a front porch.
My friends and hers
buzzed about us like gnats.

We talked about the future.
At twelve, every thought is of tomorrow.
I remember our knees would touch
now and again
like a promise.

The neighborhood spawned
moving vans and U-Haul trucks.
Those with any money at all
were fleeing to the South Shore,
to brand new split-levels
with three bedrooms
and a bath and a half.

My dad, a master of irony,
would strike a pose

and intone:
"To a little bit of heaven
on a quarter acre lot."
My family stayed.

She left in August
just before the start of school.
I'd like to tell you I kissed her goodbye
as the overloaded van
sat idling on the avenue,
Mozart played Requiem on our baby grand,
and the Brooklyn sky
sported both sun and moon.
But, I suppose, you might not believe me.

Chessmaster

In our family of hard hats,
Uncle Arthur sported a beret
and a Goodwill tweed,
sipped cognac from a hip flask,
decorated like an accouterment
to the Queen of the Nile,
and proudly went by the nickname
Inka Dinka Do,
because of his enormous schnoz
and his other-worldly wit.

Arthur lived in sin
with the Countess Natasha.
They made a striking couple.
She was twice his height,
dressed all in black,
and spoke a hybrid
Russian-Rumanian-Hand Gesture dialect,
difficult to render to English.
Yet, she was as warm as flannel pajamas.
They lived in a cold water flat
near Washington Square Park
where Arthur hustled chess for a living.

He played as many as 20 games
at a go, humping from table to table
like a mad scientist, blinding underlings
with his undeniable brilliance.
People paid five bucks a shot
for the brief and painful privilege
of being beaten by the best.
He swore up and down that he only lost twice
in thirty years.
We tried hard to believe him.

My dad,
convinced I was a chess prodigy,
sent me for training
the summer I was eight.
Sooner or later all my cousins
auditioned.
Inky taught me to push pawns,
to Castle early, and to drink
the double espressos
he made every hour
in a hand press
held together by duct tape and twine.
He could tell in an instant
I'd never be the next Bobby Fisher,
but as a favor to my father
he worked with me for a week.
If I live to be a hundred
I hope never to hear the words
check or mate again.

Natasha sent me home
with a box of checkers,
and a peck on the cheek.
I may not play chess,
but I start each morning
and end each evening
with a Chessmaster's double.

Sam and Saul

The twins were prodigies
in math and music.
Saul played cello,
Sam the violin.
By the time they were three
experts were measuring
the elasticity of their brains
and listening
to their rendition
of Pachelbel's Canon
with tears in their
calculating eyes.

We preferred The Stones
to Pachelbel
and treated the guys
as if they were normal.
Mostly they were,
as long as you didn't invite
them to play poker
at stinky B's after basketball
or try to beat them
at Scrabble or chess.

Saul sickened and died
the year they were to start
at the Institute for Advanced Study.
Our parents spoke of leukemia—
murmuring "blessedly quick,"
as if a mantra to ward off evil.
They buried him on a day in March
so raw it was a relief
to be in the overcrowded synagogue
listening to sorrow

recited as it should be—
in the ancient language
of Torah.

After the service,
Sam sat all alone
in the bitter cold
outside their apartment building
and played his brother's cello.
It was the most beautiful thing
I'd ever heard.
He played through the sunset.
He played until
his father gently took his hand
and helped him up
to their half-empty home.

Taxi

My dad drove a taxi
on the night shift
through the tired streets of Manhattan,
his nights filled
with swampy coffee
and drunks
ejected from the local bars.
He'd tell the story
of the drunk that paid
his tab twelve times
in crisp twenties
thinking each time his ride had just ended,
or of the ride he gave
to Marilyn Monroe
who kissed him on the cheek
because she didn't have a dime.
But most days, he slept.
We tiptoed past him,
dead to the world
on the fold-out couch
in the living room of our tiny apartment
and tried to be so quiet.

When he had one Saturday free
he took me to Ebetts Field.
He loved the Brooklyn Dodgers—
Campanella, Hodges, Pee Wee Reese
and most of all, Duke Snyder.
We sat in the bleachers
in the blazing sun
and watched Sal Maglie
and Hoyt Wilhelm
take it to the seventh,
nothing nothing.

Dad went for hot dogs at the stretch
and came back with two for me
just after the Duke homered in the ninth
to win the game one to nothing.

We didn't speak on the train going home,
but on Sunday around the bagels and lox
he told that story with a smile and a laugh.
It was my only trip to Ebbets Field
and his last.

Sex Appeal

From his early teens
my fast friend Tom
was fluent in woman.
His at-ease-ness
with the fair sex
was so at odds
with my slight
experience,
I suspected
a pact with Lucifer.

I hung around,
hoped that one or more
budding damsel
might tire of Tom
and find my
tight-lipped stammer
and pimpled brows
appealing—
but never
a nibble.

Secretly,
I wished Tom rickets.
I wished him a misstep
on the subway platform
as the 7th Avenue Express
roared through.
I wished that Zeus
would bolt his too easy
heart and leave
him to smolder
in the schoolyard.

I Remember November, 1963

It was the Saturday
after they'd gunned
down Kennedy.
Too cold for b-ball,
we huddled
in the schoolyard
and talked
at half voice.

We didn't notice Joel
at the corner of the chain link
until he began to kick
it and scream,
"I'm so ugly."

And he was.
It was as if
he was sculpted
from a single piece of granite
by an indifferent artist
who said,
"This is good enough,"
and put it aside.

We didn't see the gun
until he put it
to his head
and pulled the trigger.

We all heard the empty click
and the wail of utter despair.

I remember that click
as clearly as I remember
that last motorcade.
And, I remember,
that even after he dropped
the pistol,
not one of us
ran to help him.

Spendthrift

After Max died,
Aunt Sarah spent
her spare time
at the Seminole Casino
near Coconut Creek.

They'd had no children
and she would claim
the slots were more compelling
than the quiz shows on TV.

It was the early '60s,
before Florida boomed,
and the half duplex
she owned in Center Village
stood, looking awkward
and embarrassed,
with fifty others
in the middle of the nowhere
that was Hillsboro Boulevard.

Each day she'd sit
with a paper cup of nickels
and feed the one-armed bandits.
She told us she'd hold her breath
while the grapes and lemons spun.
A big strike might yield $50—
the nickels erupting
to dance on the concrete floor.

Behind her back
we called her
the palest Seminole in Florida,
as she never saw the sun.

But we were young then
and hadn't yet sampled
the fruits of loneliness.

Fumarole

"You know,"
Tony said with a smile,
"they'd like
to vent volcanoes,
drill into them
to relieve the pressure.
Imagine
gas escaping
like steam
from a giant's teakettle."
We were drinking coffee
at the counter of Abe's
on Bristol Street.
Two eggs up, bacon,
and a toasted bagel.
Tony had given up
on the bagel.
He was missing
two front teeth
and his face looked like
he had lost an argument
with a Mixmaster.
He was tall and dark
with a laugh as contagious
as measles.
But somewhere,
in the tangled machinery
above his eyes,
he had a screw loose,
and out of the blue
he would blow.

Then, for a few
frantic minutes,
Tony was a human
wrecking ball.

Last night,
he had hunkered
out of the way
as his ex parked
her dad's car,
then he took a baseball bat to it.
Sweating and swearing,
he shattered
windshields and lights.
The dad and two friends
caught up with him later,
as he walked home alone.

"They will kill you,"
offered Abe,
"if you keep
that crap up."
Sooner or later,
I thought.
Everyone did.

"But the drilling
is more than likely
to set it off,"

Tony said,
squeezing his napkin
into a quarter-inch ball.
"The eruption,
that is," he said,
sweeping his
meaty hands
up over his head
to show
how the volcano,
when tampered with,
would blow.

Song

"He has no one to blame but himself,"
she murmured
in the rhythmic cadence of grief—
a patter as old as life on earth.
She sang softly,
yet her voice filled the pale green room
and hung in the acrid air.
We waited
for a surgeon to appear—
his consecrated hands
signing thumbs up,
thumbs down.

"He brought it on himself,"
she sang once more.
They had brought him in at 2 a.m.
shot twice—
belly and lung—
and rushed him to surgery.

"It's his own damn fault,"
she crooned in a voice
a cantor would kill for.
It was 8 now.
Saturday services had just begun
at the synagogue down the block.
The old, the young, and the damaged
chanted in an ancient dying tongue
for the world to heal itself.

"No, no,"
she began to chant
just as the door to the operating room
opened with a pneumatic hiss.

The sounds—
alien and human
mixed for a moment
in the pale green anteroom
between life and death.

Leroy

It was right after the rent-a-cop,
with his fine-tuned
sense of self-preservation,
made his tattooed self scarce,
that they came on the court,
so loose-limbed
you imagined them melting
in the August heat.
Yet their procession
seemed as inevitable as the tide.

I hadn't realized I was still dribbling
until Leroy was on me
face to face.
I had played b-ball with him
at pick-up games on Stone Avenue.
He was like some sub-atomic particle—
Leroyiam—
always moving.
He was good,
and when he went up for a jump shot
I was left defending knees.

Leroy showed me a metal Band-Aid box
full of twenty-two shells
and a taped up pistol
as ugly as Brownsville.
He told me,
"I'd stay off the streets tonight."

36

Soon after
the draft started
to round up the basketball stars,
the craps addicts,
and the layabouts
from the bowling alley.

Word was
Leroy flushed
his subway token
and took off
with just his basketball
and his dad's pay envelope.
They haven't caught him yet,
and the smart money says
they never will.

Perhaps, he will
grow old
and prosperous—
on a court somewhere,
lofting one-hand set shots
over his grandkids' heads
and catching only net.

For Nothing at All

I took chill last night in the rain,
and remembered how you
would always catch cold in June.
You'd sit in your living room
on that overstuffed sofa,
afghan pulled up over your nose
like the Queen of Ditmas Avenue,
exotically scented by Vicks VapoRub.

I remember the old black rotary phone
you used to call each of your many girlfriends
to complain of your impending doom—
so young, so young—
as your doting mother brought you tidbits
and fragile cups of peppermint tea,
and your brother Bob, my best friend,
made a perfect pest of himself.
I used to think
Bob was put on earth to entertain.
He could sing.
He could dance.
He could do all those happy things
I was no damn good at.

Before he left for Nam,
Bob borrowed the lucky silver dollar
that had seen my dad through his war.
On his last night home, I swore
it would keep him safe
and that I would look after his sister.
But, we lost Bob there, at 19,
in a war about nothing, for nothing
at all.

And Sue, the girl I worshipped
runny nose and all,
tried to teach me
to forgive myself.
But the lessons never took.

I still hear from her
on my birthday.
It's in June,
and it makes me smile
to listen to her speak
through a wad of tissues
and a stuffed-up nose,
and to picture how she tries but fails
to stifle even a single sneeze.

Breakdown

On that endless day in February
when I found out
you wouldn't be coming home,
I hitched a ride to Lewistown
in a car so beat up
it might have been lifted
from a junkyard on Route 220.
The delinquents that drove it
were thoroughly stoned
and moved in fractal time—
abruptly, like mechanical dolls
wound for infinity.
We took the grade
down Seven Mountains sideways,
laughing at fuck knows what.

They tossed me out
at the train station
just over the river—
a place so desolate and cold
the vegetation that grew there
could not be found
anywhere else on earth.
I sat on the icy asphalt
and cradled my backpack,
as if the contents—
some ludes and librium,
two nickel bags,
rolled sweat socks,
and a stuffed dog named Lucky—
could save me from the setting of the sun.

The train rolled through the heartland
of tarpaper shacks

and graveyards
lit by a macabre moon
made orange by train windows
crazed by the cold.
Outside, packs of hounds
hunted and howled,
prey and people fled,
and at the service plazas—
little Meccas of civilization
in the wind-blown wild—
the wretched of the earth
sobbed in the artificial light.

In Harrisburg,
a G.I. in full battle gear
sat down beside me,
stinking of blood and jungle,
his right leg lopped off
just above the knee—
the bone whiter than fresh snow.
A chest wound
the size of Ali's fist
bled on the seat.
What was left of his name tag
read PFC Deuts.
He smoked weed and told stories
of little towns in the Mekong
he had blown away
in a voice as green and sweet
as honeyed tea.
In Philly, he shot out a window
and left the train
through the gaping wound.

My brother met me at Penn Station.
Sturdy and sure,
he was dressed as a Hassid—
payot graying around his ears.
He knelt on the grimy station floor
and davened
to the beat of a hit song
as ugly as 1968.
With prayers as mechanical
as the patter of
a ventriloquist's dummy,
he sold peyote
and cheap copies of the New Testament
to travelers
desperate to get high.

Archangel

We called her Alice
because she could get
anything you want.
Names didn't matter then.
Her parents would not have recognized her anyway.

Alice lived in that condemned house on Allen Street.
You climbed in through a window on the alley.
I tried to sleep there once,
but the walls moaned
as if the house were alive.
All night, I could hear
the newly dead climb the crippled stairs.

A tape of Jim Morrison singing,
". . . this is the end . . ." played
so often in that house
you might come to believe he lived there.
And at night, in the dim light,
you had to watch where you stepped
because the trippers, the lovebirds, and the junkies
sprawled any which way on the splintered floors.

Alice, a lapsed Catholic,
wore a St. Raphael medallion
and kept a drawer
full of multicolored meds.
I brought a friend there once—
bad trip. She was just a child, really.
Alice tried to bring her down
with barbies and baby talk,

but she never made it
all the way back.

The cops came in force in '69,
took a battering ram to the front door,
dragged the hippies out into the sun,
watched as they scattered
like a litter of feral cats.
We found the St. Raphael medallion
in the gutter across from the house,
but we never found Alice.

The Home Front—3/16/68

She couldn't have been
more than 19 or 20.
When I looked closely
I could still see
the little girl in her.

She'd spent the day
recruiting for SDS
and now
was holding court
in the basement bar
on the avenue
that separated town and gown.
The evening's
protest had dissolved
into beer and peanuts
as it always did
for our group
of graduate students
dressed in radical drab.

She was smiling,
her hands speech-rhythmic
in the half light
as she presided over
a dissection of my life.

She pictured me a coward
nineteen different ways—
my research evil,
my deferment a cop-out—
as my former friends
sat drinking and smoking,
and shaking their hairy heads

as if the gift of great wisdom
had been miraculously
bestowed upon them.
I was no match for her.
She was sharp
as an acid etch.
My stammered protestation
Sounded, even to my ears,
like a confession.
And, of course,
she was right.

At 2, we stacked the chairs
on the tables and filed out.
It was cold and clear.
A million stars seemed
poised to tell us
something magical
as that wisp of a girl
marched them off—
a ragged band
of the righteous
in combat boots—
leaving me
to the silence
of the streets.

I turned up the collar
of my beat-up corduroy coat
and began to walk
cross-campus.
It would be mid-morning
before I'd finish
this set of experiments.

II

The Year We All Got Cancer

Winter stayed.
The April rain so cold
it left blisters of ice
on an earth
as scarred and pockmarked
as a landscape mired in war.

We waited through the freeze and thaw
for some sign from the recalcitrant earth,
anxiety growing with each passing day.
The sun was of little use,
peeking indifferently
through the skeletal clouds
as if late for an appointment
on another planet.

We had become
a shivering muddle—
a people resigned to winter
when we woke one day
to wild things bursting—
fields of dandelions
and mustard greens and,
in the most desolate spot of all,
a stand of wild asparagus.

At the Bay

We were sitting
at Liman's
in Sheepshead Bay,
right on the water,
which was lapping
over some fashionably
placed rocks
with the regularity
of a metronome.

He was gabbing—
he had the gift—
timing the movement
of his ink-stained hands
with the patter of his speech.
We had been eating
and drinking for two hours,
and I was worried
about the tab.

The gaslights came on
as the sun set,
and in the warm light
I could better see how old
and frail he was.
He was the Great Uncle,
the family stain,
the outlaw-artist-etcher
who passed paper—funny
money—and served time
inside, every decade.

But, he was charming,
and I was smitten.

I could tell
from just his cadence
he was family.

He left for the Men's
just as the check arrived.
A back way out,
I thought, staring at a bill
half the size of my mortgage.
But he was back in a flash,
snatched the check from
my trembling hands,
gave me a wink,
and the waiter
five crisp Franklins.

He whistled
"Stormy Weather,"
as we walked away—
the song grandpa
would whistle
when content.

Stan

He looked as if
he'd never caught a break,
worn through—in need of a shave
and a shower
and a hundred other things
only money could buy.
His lifeless eyes looked through me.
The knife was real enough.

Junkie,
I thought.

He recognized me first.
"Potsy," he said softly,
using a nickname
I hadn't heard in years.
"Stan—Stan the man,"
my voice rippled with relief.
Stan held every record
in high school track.
It was a wonder
to watch him run.
He joined the Rangers
right out of school—
Nixon sent him to Nam.

He lowered the knife,
and there, on an unlit
street corner in lower Manhattan,
we shot the shit about the old days—
of Brownsville and the guys.

We didn't pretend
we'd stay in touch.

To see him on his way
I emptied my wallet
and gave him thirty-one dollars.
It would help him
do up once or twice.
The twelve hundred bucks
I earned in that night's poker game
stayed hidden in my shoes.

I hailed a cab on East Broadway
and had it take me
the four blocks home.
It wasn't until I
climbed the stairs
and flipped on the light
that I began to shake.

At the Edge

"The important questions
have no answers,"
my friend told me.

The others had wandered off
while we sat looking out over the lake,
gone gray in the early evening light.
He spoke with little conviction,
as if hoping I might contradict him.

Every now and again
a car passed unseen
on the road behind us,
breaking that stillness
you find only in graveyards
and at the water's edge.

He knew, of course, I wouldn't.
We'd been having
this conversation
since we were teens
and shared a street corner
in south-central Brooklyn
with a gaggle of wannabe thugs.

Quite suddenly
a hundred nesting birds
took to the air.
The sky raged

as they voiced their
indignation.
Then just as suddenly
they settled,
and we sat back down,
grinning with spent shock.

Our companions reappeared
as if strolling out of the setting sun,
and as we clamored
into my weathered car,
speaking of a movie
and perhaps some dinner out,
clouds gathered and darkened.
Tonight, it might well rain.

Pyre

The image is of a man,
thirtyish I suppose,
dressed in the discomfort
of his day—hat, tie, jacket.
His is one of the photos
my mother saved
in a cardboard box,
each labeled cleanly
on the back
with only a date.
This one reads
September 4th, 1934.
There is no name.

I am intrigued
by its absence—
an uncle?
A friend?
He looks like a heavy
in an Edward G. Robinson movie.
I imagine he wandered
the grand boulevard
of Brownsville—
Pennsylvania Avenue,
a slum then and now—
up by the elevated train.
His fists clenched
as if looking ahead to trouble.
His temper awry.
The smoke
from his Lucky Strike
worrying his eyes.

On this quiet evening
in November
I add his to the stack
of photos I take
to the living room fireplace.
I burn them one by one—
it seems somehow fitting.

The gangster puts up
little resistance.
He silently browns
and burns.
Yet a plump woman
in a squirrel coat
with my mother's
wide-set eyes
burns
with fierce blue flames
and nerve-shattering pops.

The last photo,
that of an infant
in a knitted cap—
pink or blue?—
must be coaxed into flame
for by now, the fire
has burned low in the hearth,
and through the unshaded window
I watch as night comes on too quickly.

Your Birthday Would Be this Week

Just past the tunnel
the road rises,
and from its crest
I see the lights
of an entire city
shine like memories
of a life left.

When did we last
really talk,
my brother and I?
Even here,
we settle into roles
enshrined by childhood.
You play the tough guy
in a bad B movie,
and I become
the simpering sidekick.
Our patter is so to script
we manage not to mention
the hospice team,
the feeding tube
and morphine drip
that keep your heart
barely beating.

It is nearly morning
when I reach the turnpike,
and the road
seems suddenly unfamiliar.
It is only then I realize
the lights of the city
have gone out.

What I Had Forgotten

Spring came on reluctantly this year—
like the probing of a diffident lover,
uncertain of welcome.
It gave me time to remember
how much the heat of the new sun
felt like a caress,
and how the breeze from the south
made me feel like shedding layers—
clothing and skin—
and running wild-hearted
through the first green.

The Way We Are Now

My neighbor Matt
will build a fence this spring.
I watch as landscapers
pace the boundary
between our quarter acres,
penciling distances
and slopes, in hope
of a winning bid.

Frost wrote, "Good fences
make good neighbors,"
but neither Matt nor I
keep cows—
and I am pleased
when his old dog Mutt
comes to call,
expecting as his due
a belly rub and bacon.

Matt and I
have shared this line
for more than thirty years.
With our children—
close as cousins—
grown and gone,
he has taken to the iris
as I have taken to the rose.
By mid-spring the view
across our yards
"could make the centerfold
of Gardening News,"
he'd say with a chuckle,
when we two still spoke.

The fence will cost us hours of light,
and with our curse of clay and climate,
we may well lose the iris and the rose.
I fear next spring I'll mourn along the fence line
and wonder how we came to be
two gardeners who cannot even talk about the weather.

As One

Only yesterday, I found
the seeds you bought me
on a sagging basement
shelf—miraculously dry.

There was no note—
might one have said,
"With these, the past and present
exist simultaneously?"

There are dozens of packets—
a well deep with flowers to bed,
many with names
and shapes I do not know.

I will plant them as closely
as we were once.
A skein of color so entangled
it dissolves with distance to a singular blaze.

Untethered

We all knew something
was not quite right with Mike.
What sprang from his mouth
had him spending more time
in the principal's office
than in the classroom
and angered the older kids,
who would periodically lay him out
in schoolyard beatings.

1967,
the year we turned 16,
he climbed the fifty-foot maple
just outside the post office
and neither his father's threats
nor his mother's tears
could convince him to come down.
The fly-catchers got him
and took him upstate
to the red-brick asylum
on the river.

Mike told me once
he felt as if he had left
all solid ground behind.
"On good days I was drowning—
sea-slimed and salted
on a relentless ocean.
On bad days I fell through the sky
like a kite some distracted child
had let fly off
to be steered untethered
by a sorcerer's wind.
I fell and rose,

65

and fell again."
He got worse after he returned
though I didn't stay to watch.

I see Mike now and again
downtown.
He lives in the half-way house
at the bottom of Gray's Hill
and runs errands for a local restaurant.
We sometimes reminisce
for a moment or two
on the busy sidewalk.
Gentled now by the years,
he always has a kind word
and asks about old friends
while I search his weary face
for the child I once knew.

How We Fail

Phytophthora,
I learned today,
is from the Greek
and loosely translates
as "plant destroyer."
From the genus
Oomycetes or water molds,
it rots away the fine roots
of unsuspecting trees and shrubs
and then, they topple.

Last spring
we lost four oaks
in Holmes-Foster Park
after the kind of storm
that had the dog tail-tucked,
slinking under the bed
and me thinking I might join him.
Walking past the next day,
I saw the four
laid out like corpses—
spring buds not yet informed
their host had died.
I felt that something indestructible,
like Greece or Rome,
had collapsed
and marveled at the strength of storm—
though now I've learned

they were brought to earth
by microscopic mold.

My dad often said,
"don't sweat the small stuff,"
and never cared to know
the name of the microbe,
Klebsiella, that killed him,
or that its name derives
from Edwin Klebs.
Uninformed,
my dad preferred to play out
his last days at gin rummy,
at the wrought iron table
so rust-consumed
it stood by strength of will.
A penny a point
by the steaming,
sun-drenched pool.

Comfort

There was never a formal
treaty between Mom and Smokey.
For years, they recognized
the dread and dislike they inspired
in each other, and surprise
encounters, in the narrow hallway
of our old house,
provoked
arched backs,
hooded eyes,
and hissing and spitting.

So alike—
they ruled
with a surety
that brooked
no insubordination.
So different than Dad—
a gentle soul
who seemed his best
with cats and dogs
and small children—
how could Smokey
not love him?
When Dad died suddenly
one ordinary winter day
the two discovered grief,
and enmity was forgotten.

Mom and Smokey took to
sharing Dad's overstuffed wing chair
by the sunny window—
comforting each other
in unbroken silence
like old, fast friends.

Estranged

I happened by the old house today.
It was early evening,
and the well-worn sun was just beginning
to retire behind the tree line.
It had been years and years,
and I almost passed it by.

It has been poorly kept.
Someone painted the front door
fire-engine red—
which seemed to me a cry for help—
but even that has faded.
The majestic beech that towered
over the street is down.
With hands linked
we could barely get our arms around it.
I remember autumns when the leaves
pooled yellow—
inches deep on the front lawn,
how we would wade in them.

Once,
I thought
that tree would last forever.
But all things change,
even the continents
are drifting apart—
are becoming strangers.

A Death in the Family

We hustle it all to the dumpster—
couches and chairs,
lamps, rugs and bedding,
the knickknacks
that fought
for space
on every flat surface.
It's just stuff now,
and we'd like to clear the place
in time for lunch
and an early flight home.

Stories inhabit our belongings
and make them dear.
And you were so good at the telling,
your face softening with delight
as you'd describe a complicated deal
involving your great uncle Saul,
a second-hand store,
and a horse-drawn cart.
It made the rickety dining room table
seem like a gift from the Romanovs.

For a minute,
I think of my home
and wonder
how long it will take the kids
to empty it.
But this is no time for reflection.
The sleep sofa
is heavy and oddly weighted,
and the dumpster seems
farther away with every load.

A Retirement

It leafed out absent-mindedly
this year, our junk maple.
A street planting from the fifties,
its branches bald and barren here and there,
though not alarmingly so—
just enough that you would notice
if you were the kind who'd notice.
It will weather this year, I imagine,
and most likely the next,
but I worry about
our foreseeable future.
On this spot, a twig of a thing,
staked out against the bare breeze,
stands in the unshadowed sun
while from this old house, some
other someone will watch it grow.

Onion Snow

On campus, we have
retained a few stately
trees, buds just forming
forty feet above the
stone gray concrete
path I use to make my
way to class. I leave
my prints upon the
leavings of the last
snow of the season—
an onion snow we
called it once—the slow
and graceful down-
fall of large and downy
flakes that always
coats the walkways, as if
the winter had thrown
in a towel so large it
hugs the whole near
world—the path, the
trees, and the children's
hair as they march
doggedly wherever.

My prints will melt
with the snow before
the sun sets tonight.
The children will
vanish with the season.
And I, snowy hair
suddenly in fashion, old
coat buttoned to hide
my naked neck from frost,
hearing gone, sight slight,

feel as if I have walked
these old gray paths
forever, and will forever
still. That tree and I,
silly in our coats of snow,
are old friends by now,
and by the grace of god-
knows-what, we both
have been retained
to welcome yet
the greening of
another spring.

Lion's Breath

At yoga yesterday,
while downward dogging,
our instructor asked us
for five rounds of lion's breath.

It's easy—
when you exhale, stick your tongue
out as far as it will go
and with the gruesome face
that pose ensures
make the most godawful
rasping noises.

After two repetitions
I began to laugh.
I thought how wonderful
my father would have found the practice.

I imagined him lion-breathing
on the checkout line at Walmart,
during a sappy love scene
at the local twelve screen,
and at the insomniac's gin game
under the lights at Century Village.
He'd teach technique to every child
that crossed his path,
and one hundred years from today,
his descendants would still be
disrupting kindergarten nap time—
picture the peals of pure joy,
as a room of five-year-olds
discovers lion's breath.

The Dying of the Light

We found my mother
on the third floor
of a hospital
that should have been shuttered
in the 80's.
The lights were dim,
and the walls and halls
so covered in filth
it seemed they
had absorbed the misery
of the past 30 years,
and the anguish would no longer
wash away.

It wasn't hard to find mom.
She screamed, "Help me"
every couple of minutes.
We heard her from the elevator
above the endless beeping
and the garbled sounds
from the PA system.
The fact that we
were now with her
did not alleviate her need to scream.
Nor did reasoning.

She had fallen again
and broken her tailbone.
She was 95 and failing,
and I was the good son—
the one who answered the call
at 2 a.m,
booked the 1000 mile trips,
and tried to find a place

where she could end her days
in comfort.
It was rewarding in an exhausting way,
finding, unexpectedly,
I was the one to be counted on.

But, listen,
there is just so much
we can do for one another.
There are limits to prerogatives
of blood.
We practice love,
not magic,
and when
in a moment of lucidity
she stared at my face—
a face she had known
my whole life—
and said,
"I'm dying.
Save me,"
I was again
as helpless
as the infant
she had held
to her breast.

Urban Redevelopment

They took down the tenement
I was a child in today.
We were all at the demolition—
the adults slouched in lawn chairs
and shrouded in a haze of Lucky Strikes,
Viceroys, and Pall Malls.
They guzzled coffee by the gallon
and shared gossip and good-natured lies
in whispery voices so indistinct
it seemed they must be speaking of events
of great moment.

The kids ran the edge of supervision
reined in by an occasional
"Don't hit, Johnny,"
"Gloria, stop crying long enough to catch a breath."

My best friend Marvin was "it" in Red Light Green Light.
Girls played hopscotch and jumped rope,
and my long-dead brother, a waif in short pants,
was already ogling the pretty girl from 4A
who was just old enough
to be checking her reflection in a mirror
every minute.

The Kleins strolled by arm and arm.
My mom and I would visit them
on Sundays for tea and radio concerts
from Carnegie Hall.
And the couple that lived above us
stomped past
with their four oversized children
I knew collectively as Godzilla.

I'd almost forgotten how happy we were there.
We demanded so little of place,
so much of home.
If we lacked heat in winter,
we huddled.
If it was too hot in summer,
we crawled out on the fire escape
and pretended to be camping.

I shook off the apparition
and stood in the rain
dripping from the blue-black sky,
hands deep in the pockets
of my old corduroy coat—
patchy gray hair lapping my collar.

Neither loud nor dramatic,
the building collapsed with a sigh,
the debris settling in on itself.

I didn't stay to watch them
haul it away.

DNA

Writing
in the dim
and narrow light
of the old lamp
that graces
my basement desk,
I realize
once again
how I've come
to resemble you.

In a room made
mysterious by shadow,
I remember how
you would often
prepare dinner
in the uncertain light
of late afternoon,
delaying as long as you
might the incandescence
that left you oddly anxious.

I turn off the lamp
and make my way
across the dusky room,
chuckling at the skill
you passed to me,
of finding my way
in the dark.

Reunion

The night we decided
to meet, no matter what,
on winter solstice 2018,
Artie got so wasted
he couldn't figure out
how to get out of the stall
in Shadows, our local bar,
and tiny Alice,
lithe as a gymnast,
had to climb over and free him.
We carried him home
to a fourth-floor walk-up
on Calder Alley.
I kept dropping his right leg,
which left glyphs
in the fresh snow
to be interpreted
by those who'd later pass.

Those were glorious days,
the future—left unsaid—
was on everyone's lips
and seemed somehow undimmed
when Ray's F-4 Phantom
belly-flopped into the South China Sea
and Barbara lost her life
to a mole gone rogue.

I never made much of my future—
never left this college town—
worked every odd job
you might imagine.
How I loved the calls and cards

from New York, L.A.,
Paris, Singapore—
mates, careers and kids,
though they dwindled through the years
to the occasional surprise.

How I longed for our reunion,
though I should have been forewarned
when Shadows closed last year.
I stood beside the raw construction site
that frigid solstice night
stamping my feet
and blowing on my aching hands
as the whole gang arrived
just before midnight—
youthful, apple-cheeked and
full of the future.

About the Author

After a glamorous childhood in Brownsville, Brooklyn, Steve settled in State College, PA. He and his wife, Karen, have one son—the guitarist for the avant-garde group, Gang Gang Dance. Steve has spent many years as a professor at Penn State University, studying the fluid dynamics of heart assist pumps, mechanical heart valves, and drag reduction. But since retirement, he has developed a love for poetry, and over the last few years, he has published in more than two dozen print and online literary journals. He was nominated for Pushcart Prizes in 2017 and 2018. His chapbook *Perhaps You Can* was published in 2019 by Kelsay Press.

www.ingramcontent.com/pod-product-compliance
Lightning Source LLC
Chambersburg PA
CBHW022015080426
42733CB00007B/614